TREY KENNEDY

With Over 1 Billion Views Across Social Media

DADS BE LIKE

'Tis the Season to be Swaggy

Published in Pasadena, CA by Aloha and Rain, LLC. Aloha and Rain, LLC titles may be purchased in bulk for educational, business, fund-raising, or sales promotional use. For information, please e-mail info@alohaandrain.com.

The Library of Congress Cataloging-in-Publication Data is on file with the Library of Congress ISBN-13: 978-0-578-41483-6

ACKNOWLEDGMENTS

First and foremost I want to thank you. You who are reading this. You who have followed me on Vine, Instagram, Facebook, Twitter, or YouTube over the past five years. You who have taken time out of your day to give to me and my content. You who have left me a like, comment, or kind message. It means the world. And I take the privilege of (hopefully) entertaining you very seriously -- I will do it as long as you allow me. I am grateful.

Next, I would like to thank Jeff Bethke and Craig Gross at Aloha and Rain for helping birth this idea and then bringing it to fruition. You both inspire me. Thanks for believing in me.

Finally, I would like to thank my family and close friends for so closely following along with my journey and supporting me. Your random texts of encouragement or your kind words about my new endeavors mean more to me than you know. Thank you.

Love,
Trey

INTRODUCTION

Dads and dad jokes have been as much of an inseparable reality as Kardashians and athletes. Dads love trying to be funny. Emphasis on *trying*. I think it's time for an update.

Starting on the Vine app in 2014, I posted my first dad video that went on to surpass 50 million views. I have been creating content online ever since with my dad character prominently featured. It has garnered hundreds of millions of views amongst several dozen different videos posted across social media. Taking the classic corny dad stereotype we all know and love, I "milliennialized" it through video. And now I'm doing it Christmas style through my first book. I hope you like it. If you don't, well then at least recycle it, Ebenezer.

So as you turn the page to begin this Christmas edition dad book, may your reading be merry and bright. After all, 'tis the season to be swaggy.

Call me a Christmas carol because I'm taking Noel's!

DADS AND NAPS

"I was resting my eyes!" Not sure why dads are so determined not to admit they were asleep in the living room. Sorry, dad, but I do not understand how your eyes are at rest while your uvula repeatedly wallops your palate creating sounds likened to a wood chipper. I'm calling your bluff.

Dads love naps. And there is not a more guaranteed occasion for naps than the days of the Christmas season. You know once dad sits himself down in the living room after the holiday lunch feast he will be out quicker than your little brother receiving anesthesia. If you have a dad who doesn't doze off after the Christmas feast or during Christmas day football, that is a cyborg, and you need to contact your local authorities immediately.

"9-1-1, what's your emergency?"
"Hello? Yes, my dad just ate both turkey legs and half a pecan pie and is sitting perfectly awake in his recliner."
"Sir, we don't take lightly to prank calls."
"He just said I could have the remote."
"RUN!"

Speaking of remote, if you want to wake up your dad, just about any amount of noise won't do it. You know what will? Simply change the channel. In an instant, one of his eyes will open, and he will command you turn it back because he was "watching" that. Before even the next snap at the line of scrimmage, snoring will resume. Dads can sleep through the apocalypse but will regain consciousness immediately for the following:

- The channel being changed.
- The thermostat being changed.

Dad naps are a skill. It is a level of rapid mind alteration that would leave Buddhist Monks marveling. Yogis everywhere should study their abilities. Such talent has to have a more in-depth explanation; I think it may be an evolutionary technique developed to block out chattering wives and rambunctious children for, ultimately, their survival.

"Okay honey, all my family and the kids will be here for several days straight!"
Dads' evolved bodies: "I will be awake only 8 hours per day for this."

Life saved.

Throughout history, it has often been the dad who goes out and works, provides, and brings home the bacon. However, it appears that eating more than usual and doing absolutely nothing on the holidays amongst family, leaves them completely incapacitated. But it is hard to imagine the Christmas season without all the dads gathered together in sleepy unison like a small crew of docile cows. Don't worry -- they will wake eventually.

"That was a nice catnap!"
If a cat slept that hard, it would never wake again.
"I'm feelin' as fine as a feline!"
Maybe naps are also a recharge of the joke muscle.
Here we go...

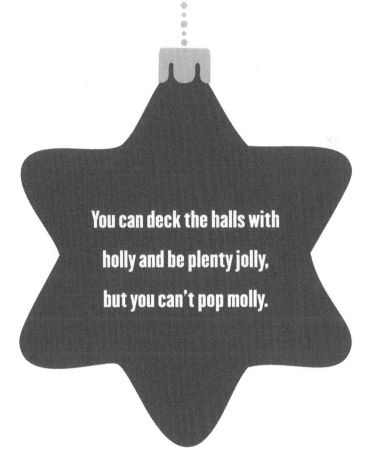

You can deck the halls with holly and be plenty jolly, but you can't pop molly.

02

I heard you kids made the nice list! What's that like? I've been one bad dude since day one.

Fa la la la la, la lose the 'tude!

Want to help me hang
the holly son? I know
it'll be the first thing
with a girl's name you
have ever touched!

05

Help me get this fire smokin'! And that better be the only smokin' you're ever doing.

DADS AND PRESENTS

Nothing says Christmas like your dad getting his annual case of golf balls and sporting around his new LED, adjustable, may be necessary once every five years, head torch for the entire afternoon; in his pajamas looking like a sleepwalking coal miner. Suddenly actual home lighting is not needed because how much more impressive is a changeable light strapped right to your fivehead?!

"Can you check on the turkey for me dear?" mom calls out.
"Of course honey!" *Turns on headlamp* *Peers into oven*

Not sure what dads' affinity is with these contraptions, but they love them. I personally do not see the reasoning for so often strapping on a light that makes you look like the "I" in "PIXAR" but what do I know? I once walked in on my own father ironing his shirt with the apparatus on. If there are two things dad loves its gadgets and frugality. Got to have that headlamp, but it sure can't be a waste of a gift. Let's use it to illuminate the morning paper!

To help those who are victims of dads headlamp gifting, I'd like to forewarn you. Here is a list of places/situations where dad may be tempted to strap on that brainbox beacon:

- At a dimly lit steakhouse.
- Candlelight service.
- Shower (if waterproof, must be tested).
- Anytime he tries to Facetime you.
- Any activity after dusk.

So, if somehow your dad doesn't already own this beautiful skull sunbeam, I'm sure he would love one. Just be prepared to walk amongst cyclops for a while after that. Hey, it's Christmas after all! Loving those closest to you despite their flaws. Dads just may be easier to spot...how ironic.

Son, you're single and
ready to mingle, but
the only action you get
is sitting on the lap of
Kriss Kringle!

07

This egg noggy got me feelin' foggy! Turn up!

08

Know what you need
to get that girl under
the mistletoe? A pair
of jingle bells!

09

Want to get the fireplace going? Just toss my mixtape in there!

10

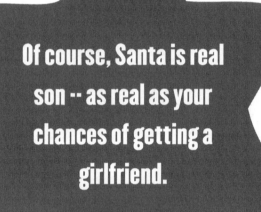

Of course, Santa is real son -- as real as your chances of getting a girlfriend.

11

Not sure which
has more ice -- the
trees outside or
my wrists.

12

DADS AND CHEESE

Every day after work, my dad would go into the fridge and cut off a piece from the block of sharp cheddar sitting perennially by the milk and eggs.

"You want a hunk of cheese?

If I had a nickel for every time my father asked me that (which I may have obliged four times), I would have a lot of money. Probably enough to buy a wheelbarrow's worth of cheese. Which would last my dad a week.

And around the Christmas season? It's like the Kraft Cheesasaurus Rex is one of our holiday guests. Dads love cheese. While cheese is always present in a Dads home, it's next level this time of year. Christmas is a time of treating ourselves and those we love, right? Well then bring on the holiday Havarti! I'm pretty sure most dads Christmas motto may be something like: Jesus is the reason for the season, followed closely by cheesin'.

Dad eating cheese "Sorry I'm being so *cheesy!*"

"Have you been a *gouda* boy this year?"

Cheeses fill the fridge and the kitchen counter but don't seem ever fill their stomachs. It's really quite amazing. And there is no limit to the type or form of cheese for dad. Cheese ball? Kobe! Shredded parmesan? Make it rain. Wheel of cheese? Roll it over. Cottage cheese? Grab me a spoon. Liquid Velveeta? That can't be real cheese. K, so?

Oh queso, that microwaved, golden, river of cheese that dad may as well inject via IV. And my parents may offer to spice things up with some jalapenos, pronouncing the last two syllables incorrectly every time (making it rhyme with *vino*, which is funny because it's exactly what I need after hearing that gringo pronunciation time and time again).

And parmesan is the close third half-sibling to salt and pepper. That stuff goes on *everything*. When a waiter asks a dad to say "when," God help him.

"Just tell me 'when' sir."
"..."
"Ummm."
"..."
"Sir I'm getting close to grating my hand."
"When!"

And that poor Caesar not only is stabbed with the fork but drowned in dry cheese. Bring on the main course next! He'll save room for the cheesecake.

Lastly, it's tough to beat a classic cheddar. But it better be sharp!

"I work all day making that cheddar, so I get to come home and eat that cheddar!"

"What do you and this cheddar have in common kids? You're sharp!" Thanks, Dad. Your love of dairy is scary.

But, I think we can all empathize with our Formaggio loving father's. Don't get me wrong, I love a good slice of swiss as much as the next guy. Well, unless the next guy is a dad.

"You sure you don't want a slice? Hold your nose -- I'm about to cut the cheese!" Oh, dad -- you're pretty grate.

Come get some Christmas roast: you're so skinny I thought you were a twig that fell off the tree!

13

Jesus is the reason
for the season, and
I'm the boss with too
much sauce.

14

Help me put up these Christmas lights kiddos. It's going to be lit!

15

A fresh pine tree for
Christmas! Don't worry, son,
you don't have to trim it;
I know you touch enough pine
riding the bench all year!

16

Ho, ho, hope you
remember to lose
that tone with me.

17

DADS AND RECLINERS

Growing up, I believe I was loved equally by my father as the other boy and girl in the house. The girl is my sister who was younger and more obedient but nonetheless loved all the same. And the other boy in the house you ask? The La-Z-Boy.

To this day I catch myself avoiding my very own recliner because I was conditioned over the years not to sit in Dads recliner like a family corgi. I have had to retrain my brain and create new neural pathways to allow myself to sit in a recliner (it has taken years, but I have accomplished it). The only leather belonging to my father that ever graced my backside was the belt, surely not the recliner. When Dad was home, that was his throne. Dads love recliners.

Recliners are a dads right of passage. And on Christmas Day, you can count on dads to kick back in their favorite leather fold out recliner, turn the game on, bark out one, "Young man watch how you talk to your mother," and take a nap. I am amazed at how far back those things can go while maintaining balance. My dad called the full recline going into the "land luge." But if need be, dads can get out of the recliner quicker than you think. I still break out in a nervous sweat when I hear a recliner quickly fold as flashbacks of my father hopping out of his own seat to give me a whoopin' spring towards my senses like some kind of spanking PTSD.

Those beastly pieces of furniture are home to a number of different memories for dad. Dads spend a third of their life sleeping, a third at work, and a third in their recliner. Below is a list of things dad can do in their recliner:

- Sleep.
- Eat.
- Watch the game.
- Read.
- Sleep.

- Raise a family.
- Scold.
- Make (bad) jokes.
- Make a family.
- Sleep.

Recliners are a dads happy place. And Christmas is the happiest time of year. So while dad sleeps in his recliner while the game he so desperately wanted to be turned on continues in the background, just know he is as happy as he has ever been. And remember: he can get out of that thing quicker than you can change the channel.

Kiddos, you're lucky even to be getting presents considering I've been dealing with so much of your presence.

18

Son, you and Rudolph
have a lot in common:
red pimple nose and no
friends!

19

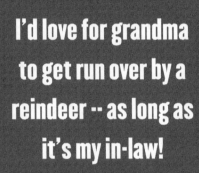

I'd love for grandma to get run over by a reindeer -- as long as it's my in-law!

20

Call me Frosty the
Snowman because
this outfit is icy!

21

Kids, if it ain't a Silent Night tonight, it's about to be a violent night. Hush up!

22

DADS AND COLOGNE

It is hard to find a more classic Christmas gift item for dad than cologne. And do not forget it is always accompanied by the classic quip, "You guys trying to tell me something?!"

No dad, we are not saying you smell bad. You asked for the Usher cologne from Ross again. Really not that big of a deal.

"Think I can smell this good and do the Stanky Leg at the same time??"

Nonetheless, the small container is passed around the room as everyone gives their obligatory oohs and ahhs as they whiff the discount fragrance. (Side note: it isn't Christmas if you aren't fake-caring about others' gifts, *especially* cologne. As if I am really dying to get a good whiff of dad right now: "Ohhh yes let me smell that! Sooooo good." Oh please.)

Most dads have that smell when you hug them where you just think, "Smells like dad." That scent you faintly sense as your brain quickly associates it to your old man, but we forget what it actually stems from -- it is all thanks to a stranger at the mall who talked him into some certain fragrance 28 years ago. Dad was probably on his way to look for a new pair of gym sneakers or a golf putter, and a pushy salesman talked your dad into buying Antonio Banderas' cologne and now that is all he will ever wear. So now Antonio Banderas cologne has to be tracked down like we are crime detectives because dad *has* to have it. Man, buying cologne stinks.

So as your dad unwraps his annual bizarre cologne, be a good sport. Put your nose up to it and inhale, smile, and say, "Smells like you, Dad."

"You want to smell something else? Pull my finger!" No thanks, Dad. I have more sense than to encourage your scents.

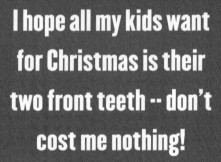

I hope all my kids want for Christmas is their two front teeth -- don't cost me nothing!

23

Carol of the Bells?
Never met her!

24

Kids, you keep talking
to me that way, we'll
have more beef than the
Christmas feast.

25

Got my new peacoat on, ready to *slay* on the sleigh!

26

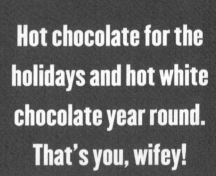

Hot chocolate for the holidays and hot white chocolate year round. That's you, wifey!

27

**Ice skating?
You kids are already
on thin ice, so might
as well.**

28

DADS AND SPORTS

Part of what makes Christmas so special for dad is getting away from the usual day-to-day, nine to five stresses and worries and surrounding him with those he loves -- with the game on.

"I really like that Steven Curry."
"It's *Steph*, Dad."

Your typical American household Christmas Day may go something like this:

- Wake up.
- Open presents.
- Eat.
- Dad turns the game on.
- Dad sleeps during said game.
- Eat more.

Combining holiday wishes with three-point swishes is a staple of many households. Sports have a way of gathering people together. They also have a way of getting dads out of the most brutal aspects of the holidays. Too much of these kids running around screaming? Let's retire to the recliner and flip on the tube. Have to talk to a stranger that is also a distant relative at the reunion and not sure what to say? Well, did you see the game last night?

We all know one of the many marks of being a dad is clouding small talk with sports talk. Sports have been saving dads from awkward conversations for generations. Every year family reunions everywhere include dads who really do not want to talk to their second cousin-in-law, but are obliged to because they are "related." (Side note: this family thing has to a have a limit to it. "What was that Mom? I *have* to talk to my step aunt-in-law because she is family?" I literally see my dentist more and even that is less painful.) But all dads can pass the time with some sports gossip if needed.

"I think Lebron really misses Cleveland...he did what he had to do."

"I always knew Kevin Durant wanted out of OKC...you could just tell."

Yeah, Dad, you know them so well. Dads love to imagine they know the inner feelings and motivations of the athlete. You don't even know what to get your own wife for Christmas; I can imagine you know the musings of NBA All-Stars. They can literally forget the anniversary to the person they have spent countless days and nights with, but memorize their favorite player's exact stat line.

"Honey, I said take out the trash," says wife. "Ahh sorry, I forgot," says dad as he mulls over the game plan for his son's next six weeks of little league football games. Which has involved reading several books on the pistol wing-T offense and watching countless hours of film utilizing different formations. All that research so a bunch of seven-year-olds can destroy their opponents when all they mainly care about is running around and sipping Capri Suns at halftime. Sorry dad, but I don't think little Brennan is any more concerned with pulling to block than he is pulling the grass out of the field.

But we can appreciate dads love for the game and how that translates to those he loves. So thanks, dads, for showing us how to play, believing in us, (one of the biggest examples of "love is blind" is dad believes their 5'7", 132-pound white son will make the NBA) and being a great head coach of the family. We might not always listen to the game plan, but we appreciate it. "Who wants to toss around the ol' pigskin?! Let's see if you still have those pan hands! Can't catch a cold!" Just tell me what routes to run, Dad. I'm open!

You know what drink
gets me movin' and groovin'?
That chardonnay nae!

29

Did you know
I speak Spanish?
Feliz Navidad!
I go loco for hot
cocoa!

30

What do you call flour
and water with no soul?
Gingerbread!

31

Wakey, wakey eggs and Drakey! It's "God's Plan" for you to get up and go to Christmas Eve service!

32

**Remember kiddos:
don't smoke trees,
decorate them!**

33

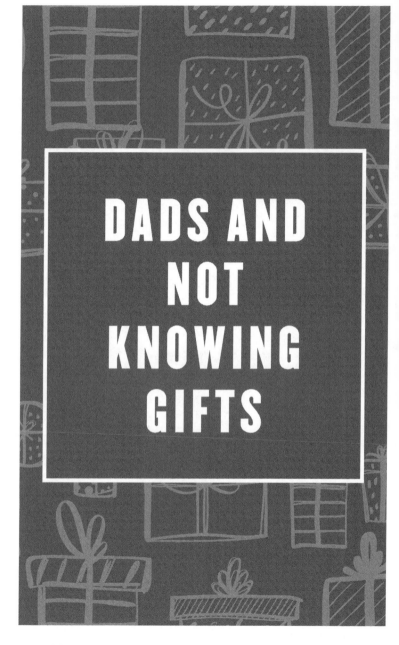

DADS AND
NOT
KNOWING
GIFTS

We all know the adage, "It is better to give than to receive." And we all love surprises. How great would it be if these were somehow all wrapped (literally) into one? Just ask a dad.

"Okay, this one is from us!" says mom. I ferociously unwrap. "Oh, what is this?!" I say as I unbox the gift. (Meanwhile, Dad is just as curious as I am to see what he's co-gifted me.) "I love this quilt with all of my high school sports shirts sewn into it. Thanks, Mom and Dad!" (Not to worry, Dad. I didn't expect you had much hand in the choosing and wrapping of the said gift.)

A dad does give some great gifts. But there are times when he forgets what he and mom picked out or altogether has no knowledge of the gift being opened. If a gift has a strong feminine tilt, there is a good chance dad had no hand in its selection and preparation.

"Thanks, Mom and Dad for this Bath and Body Works shampoo and body wash!" (Yeah, right. I know Dad wasn't in on this one. Like he could really care how my hygiene routine goes.) "You bet, son! Don't forget to wash behind your ears. Keep them clean like your dads swag!"

But it's okay dads, we are happy getting all of our presents anyway. I will know immediately who had a hand in these Lebron basketball shorts. We'll just pretend like we never knew you never knew what those other gifts of mine were. Christmas is bliss, and so is ignorance.

How about instead of
stuffing your stockings,
we stuff your mouths
with the stockings!

34

Will my son get
his first kiss this
Christmas season?
Mistle-no!

35

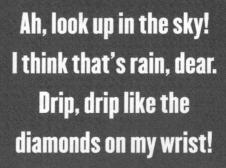

Ah, look up in the sky!
I think that's rain, dear.
Drip, drip like the
diamonds on my wrist!

36

Thanks for the gift son! Did you make it? You're short enough to be an elf!

37

Yuletide YEET!

38

**My *tidings* is that
I'm *providing*, so you
better be *abiding*
by my rules!**

DADS AND THE LIGHTS BEING LEFT ON

Growing up, I was a terribly scrawny kid. No amount of calories could add a pound to my frame. At the time, it was baffling to think my caloric intake was not surpassing my caloric expenditure. It now occurs to me this was likely caused by the uncountable amount of times I had to run back upstairs to turn the lights off.

"Is that your bathroom light that's still on? Go turn it off!"

There are a few things that have become second nature to me: breathing, blinking, scrolling past any wedding video on social media, laughing, and turning off every light switch when I exit a room, whether it is my home or not. I am alarmingly well-trained to turn off the lights.

"If the lights are lit, your behind is next! Turn 'em off!"

Dads are obsessed with having the lights off when they aren't in use. Only the lights in the room you are currently in can be on. Money must be saved! We might as well remove all the lights and each walk around the house with our own personal candle like we are medieval peasants. So when Christmas rolls around, you can imagine the panic that sets in for dads.

With guests galore, dads watch unoccupied bathrooms like a hawk. Panic surges as relative after relative leaves bedroom and hallway lights on with no purpose other than to drain his wallet of tens of dollars. Timers are set to all lights on the property. Think those Christmas lights on the house are pretty? Enjoy them while you can. That timer shuts them off at 10:00 pm sharp. Need a midnight snack? The kitchen lights shut off hours ago. You are surviving on night lights and night lights alone.

"I stay lit 24/7, but the lights don't!"

If you asked an average dad what he does on the holidays, he would say relaxing, spending time with family, but mostly making sure that all the lights are turned off. Dads love to shout things like, "Is *every* single light in this house on?" Or the classic, more passive-aggressive, "*Sure*, leave the lights on. Be my guest. Let me know how you want to pay the bill." And as we know, holidays can get stressful. Things like buying presents, wrapping them, making everyone happy can pile up on a person. But for dads, the greatest stressor is the mission to keep the family celebration as cost-effective as possible. May your Christmas' be merry and bright, but also cheap!

So, when Christmas morning comes around, and all the kids run downstairs, they need to remember one thing: lights off before you come down.

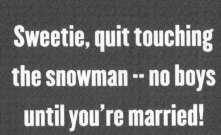

Sweetie, quit touching the snowman -- no boys until you're married!

40

**This adult apple cider
got me in a holidaze!**

41

Son, we said ugly sweater party, not face too!

42

I tell you what, the last thing I want roasted is my chestnuts!

43

The greatest gift
is family.
But the worst
gift is a family
reunion!

44

DADS AND COFFEE

Decaf Folgers. What's the point? Next page.

Outfit so cold got
me feelin' ill, call
that I-sick-le!

45

Son, you sure can't talk to bells, but at least you can jingle them!

46

What do you call a reindeer
playing defensive end?
Blitzen! But kids you better
not ever be getting blitzed.

47

Kids, keep that cranberry sauce away from me -- I already have too much sauce!

48

DADS AND TRAVELING

For a lot of us, Christmastime is a time to travel and a time to travel to nowhere glamorous; like to your grandparents in Nebraska or your cousins in Shreveport. Can't wait! But whether you are flying or driving, dads do things a certain way.

"Our flight is in four and a half hours. Let's go!"

Dads obsession with getting to airports remarkably early is beyond me. And you know that during the holiday season, that obsession will only increase.

"We have to get to the airport early; my private jet wasn't available today! I'm comedy!"

So, next thing you know you are sitting in an airport terminal with three hours to kill while you try not to kill your family. And all dad keeps saying is that is better to be safe than sorry, but you are really kind of wishing you were sorry. Perusing the bookstore at terminal 17 is only fun for so long. Card games at the table in the Schlotzsky's went 20 minutes longer than you would have liked.

"Dad, why are we here so early? Can we come back later?"
"Well you were born early, and we couldn't put you back. I guess we'll stay for this too!"

When the time finally comes to board the Southwest flight, dads always grab that aisle seat. He sure as heck isn't going to let you charge the $8 it takes to text on the WiFi. Now begins a couple hours of a sleeping father beside you while you wonder if this journey will ever end. But far, far worse are road trips.

"I got the *whip* *does dance move* all loaded up! Let's hit the road!" And as everyone walks out, dad is "hitting" the road with his hand and laughing. "Let's *hit* the road!"

The tone has been set, and it isn't a good one. As hours pass, every answer to the kids' questions will inevitably be "no."

"Can we stop to go pee?"
"Can we get McDonald's?"
"How much longer?"
"No."

But plenty of fun games are to be had. How about, let's see if the family can locate all 50 states on passing license plates? Every letter in the alphabet on billboards? (Those pesky Qs and Zs!) I spy?

Well, Dad, I spy with my little eye a bridge up ahead you can send us off. Just kidding, I still want my presents.

And as far as directions go, technology has eliminated a lot of the issues; but, it has created plenty more. First, get used to hearing Siri's voice because you will be hearing her directional advice every five minutes for the next seven hours. Next, be prepared to still hear dad argue with mom over somehow still messing up directions when a computer is verbally spoon feeding them commands. And lastly, dad will never ever tell you the answer to, "Are we almost there yet?" even though the estimated time of arrival is clearly displayed on his GPS.

Eventually, grandma Gene's house is coming just around the corner. And once you spot her familiar front lawn and her smiling face waving towards your dad lightly honking the horn; the excitement of the holidays returns. And speaking of returns, let's try not to think of the trip back.

We are about to get jolly AF this Christmas season!

49

I don't know who Mary Christmas is but have her DM me!

I don't know why we are so
excited to see snowflakes;
I've been raising a couple
of them for years! Ha just
kidding kiddos!

I like my potatoes sweet
and my wife sweeter!

52

Know what rhymes with cheer? Beer. I'll take both!

53

DADS AND TECHNOLOGY

Modern technology is a fascinating thing. All of us use different aspects of it as necessities to our everyday lives. But it is dads who use the most useless technology time and time again.

"You kids are always on those darn phones. Those Jenners and Kar-dash-uns will be there tomorrow too!"

"Honey, you want to spend Christmas with Facebooks or me?"

As dad harasses the kids and wife over the use of phones, he is setting up his new Bluetooth controlled electric meat thermometer. Or his voice-activated light bulbs. Dad, if you get to spend hours tampering with and repeatedly saying in a much-louder-than-necessary volume, "UH-LEX-UH, LIGHTS ON," I get to bury my head in my phone for a bit.

"UH-LEX-UH, WHY IS MY WIFE SO BAD AT COOKING?"
"I'm sorry. I don't know the answer to that," says Alexa, obviously.
"Ha! UH-LEX-UH, PLAY J. COLE"
"Shuffling J. Cole."
"Forget the fireplace, Alexa bringing that fire right now!"
"I'm sorry. I didn't quite get th--"
"ALEXA SHUT UP," I shout.

Dads love technology, especially the most obscure kind. How about a metal detector? Or an industrial grade blender? I don't know about you, but I do not think there is a strong need for unearthing rusty nails or having an appliance that has the strength to liquify an entire raw potato. Or how about surround sound? Do you love watching movies where the audio never works? Then just hand over your in home entertainment to the dad!

But at some level it is impressive. Dads do a surprisingly good job operating these new forms of technology, yet leave legitatemely useful technologies by the wayside. Dads can fully operate a high-tech, touchscreen universal remote that can both turn on the television and the sprinklers, but cannot manage to take a simple photo without it coming out blurry or with everyone's head in the frame. Don't worry Uncle Dale, we know what the top of your head usually looks like. We will just pretend like it's there when we reflect back all these years.

Just don't be too surprised when dad greets you at the door with his voice projecting through a security camera he controls through an app on his phone. Or that only he can now control the almighty new smart thermostat. He will still need help taking a proper selfie he will want up on your Instagram story -- just make sure you tag him.

I spilled some wine on my Christmas sweater. But don't worry! Son, you'll Tide it.

54

The only mouth I want
moving this Christmas
is the nutcrackers.

55

Son, look! Mistletoe!
Go ahead, kiss goodbye
any chance of playing
more of that fortnite.

56

The only thing that mistletoe might do for you, son, is get an extra kiss on the cheek from Grammy.

57

Bump some music in
the manger, call that a
Nae nae-tivity scene.

58

DADS AND VIDEO CAMERAS

In my family, year after year, the dads of our large family get-together videotape Christmas morning. Have I ever seen this footage? Is this footage ever used in any capacity? Do I like being videoed at that hour of the morning? The answer to all of those questions is a firm "nope."

"Okay, kids...come on downstairs!"

When we were eight years old, this was cute. I am a grown man now that has already had a cup of coffee with you this morning, Dad. Do I really need to go back up and come down for the camera like I'm a 17-year-old girl going to prom? 'Tis the season!

Have you ever noticed how much dads complain about taking photos when the moms obsess over getting the right picture in front of the tree? (Side note: moms take ten different photos with ten different iPhones. Take one and airdrop it?? Okay, back to dads now.) Dads hate taking pictures. They snicker, and eye roll at the incessant after-church photo shoot the women put us all through as the girls try to capture that perfect holiday angle. But I am eye rolling even more at your video camera, Dad.

Dads *love* videoing. I remember as a kid having to strike a pose for Mom as she snapped pictures of me post-basketball game while my dad had filled up an entire cassette tape with thrilling eleven-year-old sports footage. At least I watched that once. The Christmas footage? Might as well be any new Nicolas Cage movie -- no one sees it.

I am not exactly sure why dads disown photography but embrace videography. But with technology these days, things get even worse. Dads, please stop shooting videos with your 13" iPad. We are begging you. You have a perfectly good smaller version of that in your pocket.

"Call me iPad Dad!"

And for the ones lucky enough to avoid "iPad Dad" and get dads who video on their phones, you are bound to get an accidental selfie video from time to time. A full ten minutes of dads face. Do you not see yourself staring back at you? It's okay -- no one was going to watch it anyway!

Nowadays, I can handle it. It was the high school years that brought me near my wit's end. When all I wanted was to sleep in, I was awaked bright and early for showtime.

"Oh, look who finally decided to join us!"

Do you know the most annoying thing to hear upon waking? See the above quote.

But when that Christmas morning does come around, and you see dad roll on up with his camera of choice, try to find the holiday cheer. There is a pretty good chance he will unknowingly shoot the video in slow-mo anyway.

'Tis the season
to be swaggy!

59

Sweetie, I need you to know the North Pole is the ONLY pole you'll be associating yourself with!

60

Ah, the Grinch!! Wait,
that's just your mother
rolling out of bed!

61

I told you I want canes for Christmas: candy and pimp. Ballin!

62

Who's the thermobrat
who keeps touching the
thermostat because
you're about to get
thermosmacked.

63

Watch out, I'm about to
cut the cheese! Only gouda
kids get a slice.

64

Jesus got frankincense, but y'all are about to get *spankin*cense if you keep talking back.

DADS AND WAKING UP EARLY

"Rise and grind son!" says dad as 7:30am arrives on a Saturday morning.

"DAD... WHY?!"

My dad used to burst in my room, rip away my covers, and peel back the blinds. When that still didn't do it, I heard the bathroom water running, and that's when I began to beg for mercy. He would then proceed to dip his fingers in the cup of cool $H2O$ and flick towards my face like a form of Chinese water torture. Safe to say it was effective.

And on Christmas morning, wake up time comes early. As young kids, this morning couldn't come soon enough, but at some point, too early of a Christmas morning turns to mourning quickly -- mourning the end of another pleasant sleep. So as the shouts come up to command the kids to come see what Santa brought, we know good, and well that iPhone is in video mode ready to capture another worthless Christmas morning video.

"Didn't get enough beauty rest kids?! Call me Beyonce because I woke up like this!"

And if you ever manage to get some time to sleep in, be ready for the barrage of hate comments heading your way in the living room. Nothing gets dads triggered like sleeping past nine in the morning.

"Oh my! He's alive!"
"Good morning! Or should I say afternoon?"

And if you ever ask a dad why in the world he wants you up so early all the time, his answer will always be to "be productive." What does that mean? Do I need to start a business or something? Run a marathon? Do my taxes? I'm 16, Dad.

As exciting as the holiday break is for kids, dads will make sure they are up and at 'em. None of this sleeping in nonsense. Chores are mandatory, and they are to be done at eight in the morning. Because dad said so. That's all the reason you need (*eye roll*).

So as you lay your head to sleep at night during this joyous season, enjoy that late morning rising. Or if dad has worn off enough on you, make sure your early morning is productive, whatever that means.

Give me the remote.
I changed your diaper,
so I get to change the
channels!

66

I would love to make a
toast, but I'm gluten-free!

67

Hey everyone, let's do the whole 30! That's where you keep your hole shut for this entire month!

Son, you got a date to the Christmas dance? How much you pay her? 10 bands? 50 bands? 100 bands? Shoutout to Drizzy!

69

What do you call the sweet lady who provides you with all your holiday treats? Your motherfudger! No cursing in this house kids.

70

DADS AND THERMOSTATS

There's a lot of reasons dads love Christmas, but the bane of their existence may be the holiday fight over the thermostat. With so many visitors and guests vying for their preferred temperature, a dad will not back down.

"Dad, can we please turn the heat up?"
"Sure! Why don't you go back and pick some money off the money tree out back so we can make that happen."

And don't try to argue with that, because dads may not be willing such simple tasks as put the toilet seat down or take the trash out, but they have labored over the number crunching necessary to know exactly what that extra two degrees will cost. We all suffer to save $28.19 per month!

"Dad, it's *freezing* in here."
"Well, you're dressed like it is summer. You're fault."

Oh, I am sorry. I did not realize I need to bundle up like I'm snowshoeing across the Yukon in our own house.

"That is what blankets are for."

I think if the Snuggie repositioned itself as less of a fun blanket and more as a survival tool for the holidays at dads house, they would have the cash flow of Apple. According to dads, all of a sudden blankets are no longer a luxury comfort item, but one of necessity in enduring the harsh indoor winter.

"Dad, come on, it's set to 62."
"I think all that ice on your mother's ring finger is making it cold! The only thing we're turning up is this party! Ha!"

A cooperative mission begins: turn up the heat. Do we sneak to it in the night? Crawl over to it while dad is "resting his eyes"?

(After thinking about it, maybe dads claim they don't sleep, but rather "rest their eyes" to keep you in fear of tampering with that torture controller.) However, we all know the undertaking is futile. Dads senses are too keen to the almighty thermostat.

"I knew I smelled gas."

What? Are you a trained German shepherd? You can literally sense with your nose when someone has activated the heater? Have you spent significant time whiffing propane to prepare yourself for this situation? It is astonishing. But nothing is as mind-blowing as a dads ability to somehow be an omniscient thermostat god. Spidey's sixth sense has nothing on a Dads thermostat sense.

"Dad, it was so cold last night."
"I know you turned it up. I woke up and went and turned it back down."

I will never know how they do it. If you're dad ever goes missing, and you feel all hope is lost, and he is gone forever, and you've exhausted seemingly all options, go turn up the heat.

Text alert sounds *1 unread text from Dad* "Turn that down. You want to pay the bill?"

And these days, the smart thermostats are draining hope from all Christmas guest occupants everywhere. Dad has that app on his phone set, and it is not changing.

"You kids keep trying to touch the new thermostat, but I have the controls! Smart thermostat, dumb kids!"

Dads continue to win the war, but we will never stop battling. But that's just another one of Christmas's strange gifts -- feeling all the warmth and love from those you hold most dear while unable to feel your toes.

Nothing means being home for the holidays like hot cider and barking spiders!

71

If it's better to give than
to receive; I will gladly
give my kids away.

72

What do you call a
great smelling rapper?
Post Cologne!

Sorry, I wasn't listening
while I ate; I was a bit
preoccu*pie*d with this
dessert!

74

If y'all talk back to your
mother one more time,
I'll light you up like our
Christmas tree!

75

DADS AND BACON

During this time of year, we are no strangers to wrapping things. Yes, all presents should be wrapped in festive paper and placed under the tree. No, not everything edible needs to be wrapped in bacon and placed in the oven, dads.

"What if we wrapped that turkey in bacon? And when we're done with our son, how about the actual turkey, too?!"

Dads love bacon. Bacon only makes things better! Steaks? Wrap it. Lil smokies? Wrap it. Meatloaf? Lay that sliced pork across the top like a warm meat blanket (you've got to love that we wrap our meat in meat). Green beans? Let's wrap it in that fatty pig belly and coat it in brown sugar. Salad? Toss in those bacon crumbles baby!

"Kiddos, breakfast is ready! I have been shakin' and *bacon!*"

Everyone is home for the holidays and dad has made some eggs and bacon. The smell beckons you and your stomach growls. Hard to beat that. Easy to beat the jokes.

"How about some bacon for my *baecon?*"

Ew, Dad, quit feeding Mom.

When the morning meal has concluded and clean up begins, dads might store up some of that leftover bacon grease.

"Let's cook tonight's broccoli in that!"

And then he will dunk the meat juice soaked veggie in some ranch, and all will be well. Eating healthy is important!

At restaurants, you can count on dad to spend those extra couple dollars to add some bacon strips to that burger. And if it is applewood smoked (although he couldn't actually explain to you what that means), I assure you no amount of money is stopping him. This is why he keeps unfathomably tight tabs on thermostats and light switches. Money saved is bacon earned.

I would like to point out that as I'm typing this, I realize how I was not allowed to splurge for the strawberry lemonade (because water is free!), yet Dad was perfectly willing to pay that bacon fee. I hope he enjoyed his glorious burger while I defiantly slurped down half a glass of Applebee's tap water. But I guess I can't get too upset. Ultimately he was the one bringing home the bacon; he just ate it too.

We sing Carol, we say Grace, and we wish people to be Mary. I don't know who these gals are, but I'd like to!

76

Look kids: all these
sweet pies and you are
still being salty!

77

I don't know why you kids want a pet so bad when you already have a GOAT walking around.

I'm keeping it 100 when I say we're keeping it 58 on the thermostat.

79

Gather round kids-your mother wants to look at old photo albums! Or as I like to call them, TBT books.

80

What do you call a fat,
crazy Kriss Kringle?
Psyocpa*thicc* Santa.

81

My Christmases may be bright, but my kids sure aren't!

82

DADS AND PRANKS

I would like to play a little game I like to call "Do You Have a dad?"

Have you ever opened up a gift to unveil a PlayStation box as elation enveloped you? And you tried with all your might to quickly reveal its contents, but the tape was too secure for your joyfully trembling fingers? So your dad kindly offered his knife to cut the tape, and you opened the packaging, and all your joy left you like Santa in the night because staring back at you was a brick with a sticky note reading "gotcha"?

If you answered yes, you have a dad.

"What?! Are you surprised it wasn't a lump of coal?!"

So many of us have fallen victim to dads classic present prank. Did you ask for a new car? That set of keys is actually a flash drive. A new basketball? That's a melon wrapped in candy cane paper. New shoes? Just wait until you open up that Nike shoe box to find a pair of Crocs.

"Are those Crocs, son?! Close it up before they bite!"

Funny how dads don't have any idea what is in any of the other presents for their children (as mom took care of it) except the one he has painstakingly planned for your misery and his enjoyment. Be wary of scavenger hunt gifts from dad; those wreak of prank potential. A scavenger hunt gift from dad begins with a note in the initial gift and may proceed similarly to the following:

- "Look in the closet by the entryway."
- "Look on my Ford Fiesta's windshield."
- "Look in the pantry by the Frosted Mini-Wheats." (Dads love Frosted Mini-Wheats.)
- "Look on your bedroom light switch."
- "You don't have to pay for electricity again this year!"

Before you know it, dads booming laugh reverberates up the stairwell and into your ears, replacing any holiday cheer that may have existed there. (I mean, how often is he going to harp on this electricity thing? What did dads in the 1800's whine about? The coal bill? "Oh, another coal in the furnace! You think I'm made of money?") Downtrodden and dejected, you drudge towards the stairs to face the man himself. Dads love the pranks, but more times than not they love us more. Eventually, dad brings out the very gift we wanted -- we just had to work for it a bit.

"Now that is is a prank! We need to upload that on the YouTubes. Hashtag viral!"

Dashing through the snow? How about *dabbing*?!

83

Call me the drummer boy
because I'm checking
out your mother's pa
rum pum pum-pum!

84

This tree is holi*dank!*

85

Call me humbug in this Christmas sweater because I'm looking fly!

86

Fam, y'all are my ho,
ho homies!

87

**Our tree is real!
The only thing artificial
around here is your
girlfriend, son!**

88

I'm cooking this year!
Who cares for a slice of
Bethle*ham*?!

DADS AND
TOOLS

"Son, grab the hammer and hammer this in. And this better be the only time you're getting hammered, young man."

Dads have tools for almost any given issue (and it should be noted that this does not mean they will be able to fix any given issue). And a good portion of their stockpile is accumulated during Christmas. Tools provide a great opportunity for dad jokes to be made, so below is a list of gifts with their potential accompanying joke attempts from dad (this list is not exhaustive):

- Hammer: "You guys nailed it!"
- Screwdriver set: "Y'all sure didn't screw me over this year!"
- Level: "Hey son, get on my level!"
- Pipe wrench: "Well, pipe it up!"
- Stud finder: "Oh, looks like it's going off on me!

Tools are to a man as candles are to women -- can never have enough. But beware, all that hardware can lead a dad to believe he can fix anything. Tool giftings are a double-edged sword (don't ever get your dad an actual double-edged sword). Oh, the kitchen sink is leaking?

"Son, grab my monkey wrench!"

Pay no mind to the fact that merely days ago he barely knew what that was before it was gifted to him, but he's putting it to use. Next thing you know the family has a bigger debacle than when he began, and he has officially put the monkey in monkey wrench.

Regardless, if all else fails and you are not sure what to grab your old man this holiday season, grab him that new socket wrench set. Sure, he may shout, "Sock it to me!" upon opening it, but that just shows he loves it. So pay no mind that dad already has more tools than a Gold's Gym and give him the gift of hardware. You know the drill.

You know what
my favorite holiday
condiment is?
In Excelsis mayo.

See these sneakers fam? I'm rocking more heat than a candlelight service!

91

If ifs and buts were candy
and peanuts, your mother
can't have them because
she's doing Whole 30.

92

I'd love three French
hens; just make sure
they're single! Just
kidding honey!

93

Eleven pipers
piping it up!

94

Son, you're so small that when you take a picture of yourself, it's an elfie!

95

**Goodwill to all men and
good riddance to my kids!**

96

Do you think any
of those eight
maids-a-milking were
milking almonds?

97

'Twas the night before Christmas and all through the house, not a creature better be stirring, or I'll give y'all a reason to squirm about.

98

I'd be happy to wrap
if you need me to!
*It's your daddy, I'm the
boss, beat so phat call it
Santa Claus*

99

You know what dance
makes me happiest this
time of year? Juju-bilee!

100

STORIES
FROM
FOLLOWERS

Ashley
King George County, Virginia

My dad was such a neat freak. That being said, I believed in Santa until 6th grade. Because after staging real footprints out of ashes on the carpet and leaving half-eaten carrots/apples/lettuce on the deck, he would spend all of Christmas morning acting like he was pissed off at Santa and the reindeer for leaving such a mess.

Andrea
Gulf Breeze, Florida

We used to have a family tradition of passing out all the Christmas cards we received that year to each person in the family. We'd divide them up equally among each person, and we would go around the room and pray for each family on Christmas Eve. We'd each have like five or six cards, so we'd each have pretty long prayers to pray. One year during the prayer, we all of a sudden heard snoring and looked up to see my dad passed out on the couch. We all just looked at each other like, oh my gosh, is he serious right now?! Then woke him up and hounded him for it. It was hilarious.

Samantha
Houtzdale, Pennsylvania

My mom and I took a trip to NYC, and when we came home, my dad said he got us a tree and put it up already. He said he put a lot of thought and effort into and we were shocked. We walked into the living room and didn't see a tree, so we asked him where it was. He pointed to the window sill, and there was a little Christmas tree shaped snack cake sitting there.

Hope
Woodland, North Carolina

When we were kids, we wanted Cabbage Patch Kids dolls. However, we were broke, so my Dad stuck a cabbage on a doll and wrapped it up for us. We were not amused, but he laughed pretty good.

Cynthia
La Porte, TX

There was a year that we lost heat right before Christmas, so we all slept in the living room. I ended up waking up while my parents were putting presents under the tree. My dad came and sat beside me and told me that he and my mom tied Santa up because he was trying to steal the presents. I got up and walked around the house looking for Santa because I wanted to meet him. I went into my parent's room, and there was a chair with a rope tied around it with Santa's clothes. I went running back into the living room screaming "Santa is gone, Santa is gone." I woke up my brother and sister. My parents were dying from laughing.

Stacie
Paoli, Indiana

One time when I was around 8 years old and my sister was 12, our dad was getting ready to take us to school one winter morning. One of us girls realized we forgot our lunch inside the house as soon as we got buckled in the car. Our dad quickly ran back inside so we wouldn't piddle around and end up being tardy for school. It was about a week before Christmas break, and there was a little snow on the ground, just enough to get his shoes nice and wet and slippery. As he ran inside to grab the lunch box, he slipped and slid like he was trying to score a home run slide in baseball to home plate. He slid all the way across from one side of the living room to the other on our wooden floor, right into the Christmas tree, knocking off and breaking all sorts of pretty ornaments. And also sliding the tree about 4 feet over and knocking the tree half over. He also went crashing into a bunch of the perfectly wrapped presents our mother had just finished wrapping a few days prior. He accidentally tore open half a dozen of our Christmas presents during the incident so we could see some of the gifts we were getting. Mom ended up letting us have some of our gifts early because she didn't wanna go to the trouble to re-wrap them and you could easily see what the presents were since dad exposed them. We still laugh about this incident yearly, 25 years later! Gotta love chaotic school mornings! Our dad has always been so fun and goofy, it seemed like it could've been a scene right out of a movie!

Kaci
Ovid, Michigan

So, growing up I could NEVER sleep on Christmas Eve. I was so excited for Christmas morning and knowing Santa was coming. One year, my sister and I were supposed to be sleeping in our room. My dad peeked in to make sure we were sleeping, I didn't want him to know I was still awake, so I pretended to be asleep. He LEFT THE DOOR WIDE OPEN and went up into the attic in the hallway next to our room and pulled down every single Christmas gift from "Santa." I just laid there looking like ":D" I tried to think of every possible explanation. Maybe Santa just drops off the gifts in the attic since we didn't have a chimney? Maybe dad met Santa on the roof to help unload? Haha, from that moment I knew something was up.

Beth
Kansas City, Missouri

When I was a kid, we bought a Christmas-y looking metal tin of dog treats for our family dog. They were sitting on the counter when my dad came home from work one day, and because there was no obvious labeling as to what they were, he ate one assuming it was a cookie. He later asked us who bought those cookies, because they weren't very good. We all lost it when we realized he ate an entire container of dog treats without knowing it. He is still ridiculed to this day for it.

Jennifer
Lancaster, Ohio

A couple of years ago, my family was watching my nieces basketball game, and I asked my dad what he was watching on his phone. His response was "curling," which started the debate on whether curling is really a sport worth watching! My dad is the hardest person to buy for and guesses all of his gifts correctly every year, so it's a running joke to try and stump him. I leaned over to my mom laughing saying that I was going to order him a USA curling shirt not knowing that he had just told my mom that's what he bought me! We opened our matching gifts on Christmas Eve & busted out laughing! We had bought each other the exact same shirt from two different websites!

Katie
New Melle, Missouri

Every Christmas my dad would lug around that giant video recorder hauled over his shoulder, and we would all take turns "holding up" our gifts so he could get it on video. One year my sister gave me a pair of underwear with the words "ghetto booty" written on the butt (I was teased for having a big butt as a kid). That year when it was my turn I refused to hold up my gift, and he said: "C'mon Kate's, show us what you got!" So embarrassingly, I held it up. His face turned bright red, and he yelled, "Put that down!" He passed away 15 years ago, and I have kept these for almost 20 years for that memory. It will live on forever!

Krista
Oklahoma City, Oklahoma

My dad swore he knew how to use the Turkey fryer, then proceeded to accidentally light the entire lawn on fire. The lawn he spent the whole summer growing (in true dad fashion). Then came in and joked, "Hope you like your Turkey well done!"

Emily
Shelby, Ohio

Every year it's a tradition to go cut down our Christmas tree. One year, my mom's extended family was over and the Christmas tree fell on my great grandma. She was fine, we all laughed and thanked the good Lord we didn't kill Great Grandma. Fast forward to the following year, SAME EXACT THING happened again. Grandma lived-thankfully! Now my dad anchors the tree to the wall.

Madeline
Sandusky, Ohio

Every year, my dad creates a scavenger hunt for my brother and me to find our big gifts. We are given our first clue, which leads us to the next clue, and so on until we find the gift. Well, one year, one clue, in particular, stumped us, so we asked my dad for a hint. He couldn't remember what that clue meant either! We spent 20 minutes trying to get him to remember, but he couldn't. We didn't get our big gifts until 4 DAYS LATER when my dad finally remembered where he hid them.

Sandie
McAllen, Texas

One Christmas I asked for a pogo stick. Well, I saw what I thought was a pogo stick all wrapped up (no box, so it was pretty obvious). I got so excited, and I got in my sister and brothers faces rubbing it in that I for sure got what I asked for...you know the whole na na na na thing. Ha! I was flying high, and every day I'd walk by and make sure everyone knew I was getting exactly what my bratty ass wanted. So, Christmas morning I woke up and ran to the tree, picked up my pogo stick and ripped the wrapping paper off. I went into a complete WTF mode!! It was a steel broomstick with two wooden handles for the pegs and handles. As I looked around to see who had messed with me, my dad cracked a smile and said, "Hmmm Santa must have heard you boasting." I cried and yelled sorry to Santa, and whoever else was listening, and eventually, he gave me the real pogo stick and went on and on how it's not OK to boast. I swear I freaking hate that word to this very day! #mydadwasasavagebeast

Maggie
Beaumont, Texas

My first Christmas, Dad filmed the entire thing while sitting on the couch. He focused on me playing the entire time, not realizing that there was a mirror behind me. And reflecting off that mirror was him, recording in his robe and nothing else. My mother has that tape hidden somewhere, and no one is allowed to watch my first X-rated Christmas. Lol.

Catriona
Fullerton, California

When I was 9 years old, my dad took me to a Christmas tree farm to pick out our tree. We found the perfect one, but it was on hold for another man who went out to find an ATM and come back (they only accepted cash). My dad was convinced this was the perfect tree, so he offered $20 more than sticker price. They sold it to him. As we're leaving, the guy that went to the ATM came in, and like some kind of tree guru...just KNEW that was his tree. He immediately singled out my dad and confirmed with the salesman that it was his. He started arguing, my dad was getting more and more irritated as this guy was going off. He was screaming obscenities and threatening to call the cops (yes, over a tree). Next thing I knew, my dad set the tree down, pops a squat, lifts the tree above his head (mind you, this was an 11ft tree) and screams like the hulk "MY TREEEEEEEEE!" The guy was so freaked out, he ran from the Christmas tree lot, and we laughed all the way home.

Jordan
Layton, Utah

One year we got a Nintendo from Santa. But on Christmas Eve in the middle of the night, I got up to go to the bathroom, and my dad was camped out on the couch playing the Nintendo. When he noticed me standing there, he quickly got up and waved his hands in front of my face talking like a ghosts saying "go back to bed. This is a dream."

Andy
Scottsville, New York

One year when I was a kid, my mother had bought a train set for display that said "Noel." You had to hook each letter onto the hook to make the train. My mother, sister, and I were asked to do the tree, and my mother asked my father to put the decorations up around the house. He asked my mother, "Cindy, how does it look?" She looked around and said, "It's good John, but one thing, who the hell is Leon!?!?" LOL, he put the letters of the train backwards, and I swear I almost peed myself. I laughed so hard and from there on out every Christmas, Dad puts out Leon.

Lisa
Greenfield, Indiana

My dad gave Santa away when we were way too young!! All we wanted was a keyboard for Christmas, and my dad sent us to bed and said Santa wasn't going to bring us our keyboard unless we went to bed super quick. Five minutes later, we heard my dad playing the keyboard...like, song after song...the next morning it was labeled from "Santa." What?!?!

Lakeisha
Toledo, Ohio

One year (I believe I was 10 or 11), my family and I were sitting around talking and I told my dad I didn't believe in Santa Claus anymore. What the hell I do that for?? He told me that Santa heard me and he probably wouldn't get me anything. I totally called his bluff...until Christmas day. I woke up and was so excited to see what I got. I ran downstairs, and got to the living room and I stood there in total shock...there was a huge banner hanging up on the wall that said. DEAR KEISHA, I KNOW WHAT YOU SAID, AND SANTA CLAUS DOESN'T BELIEVE IN YOU EITHER. LOVE, SANTA. My whole soul was crushed...until he told me it was just a huge prank. I got everything I asked for!

Erin
Cincinnati, Ohio

My dad was looking for a cheap gift for a gift exchange at work. He couldn't find anything, so he grabbed a cheap frame and put this picture in it. The next year he gave a mug with the picture. Then the third year a Fathead. They stopped exchanging gifts, so he had to get creative.

Jordan

Paris, Texas

As kids, we were all so embarrassed by our dad coming outside when we would get off the school bus. One year we had a Santa sleigh with fake reindeer in our front yard. When we got off the bus that day, he was outside in nothing but his whitey tighties riding the reindeer like a bull while hollering. We were MORTIFIED. It is still one of our favorite and scarring childhood memories! LOL.

Donna

Richardson, Texas

My dad wanted to teach his five daughters how to put out a fire one year. So after Christmas, he started a fire in our fireplace, then he took an extinguisher to demonstrate how to operate it and proceeded to put the fire out. Ashes and soot flew everywhere in the family room. We were all screaming, and he calmly put the extinguisher down, turned around and said, "Every good firefighter knows how to clean up a mess." With that said, he left. We were stuck cleaning up a huge mess. We laugh about it today…40 years later.

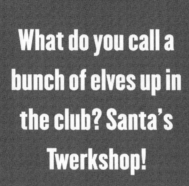

What do you call a bunch of elves up in the club? Santa's Twerkshop!

101

ABOUT THE AUTHOR

Trey Kennedy was born and raised in Edmond, OK before heading to Oklahoma State University where during his college experience, the app Vine was released. Between classes and late nights with friends, Trey created hundreds of Vine videos and quickly rose to prominence, amassing one million followers within eight months of the launch of the app.

As time went on, Trey transitioned to other platforms including Instagram and Facebook. Today he has over 3.5 million followers he actively engages through comedic content; you can find Trey across all social media platforms at @TreyNKennedy.

He now resides in Kansas City where he spends his time creating content, traveling, spending time with friends, and cheering on the Oklahoma State Cowboys, Oklahoma City Thunder, and Kansas City Chiefs.

Made in the USA
San Bernardino, CA
02 December 2018